50
KEYSTONE
FLORA SPECIES
OF THE
PACIFIC NORTHWEST

A POCKET GUIDE

———— • • ————

Collin Varner

UNIVERSITY OF WASHINGTON PRESS

SEATTLE

University of Washington Press
uwapress.uw.edu

Published simultaneously in Canada by Heritage House Publishing Ltd.
heritagehouse.ca

Cataloguing information available from the Library of Congress

ISBN 9780295752884

Edited by Warren Layberry
Cover and interior book design by Rafael Chimicatti
Cover photographs, clockwise from top left: Douglas fir by emer1940/iStockphoto; salmonberry by Collin Varner; tiger lily by Collin Varner; bigleaf maple by tntemerson/iStockphoto; lupine by Hauke Musicaloris (Flickr/CC BY 2.0); Calypso orchids by Amenohi/iStockphoto; bunchberry by dawnhanna/iStockphoto; Canada goldenrod by prill/iStockphoto.
Interior photographs by Collin Varner, except California hazelnut, p. 102, top, by Terry Howes (Flickr/CC BY-NC-SA 2.0).
Map by Eric Leinberger

The interior of this book was produced on FSC®-certified, acid-free paper, processed chlorine free and printed with vegetable-based inks.

28 27 26 25 24   1 2 3 4 5

Printed in China

CONTENTS

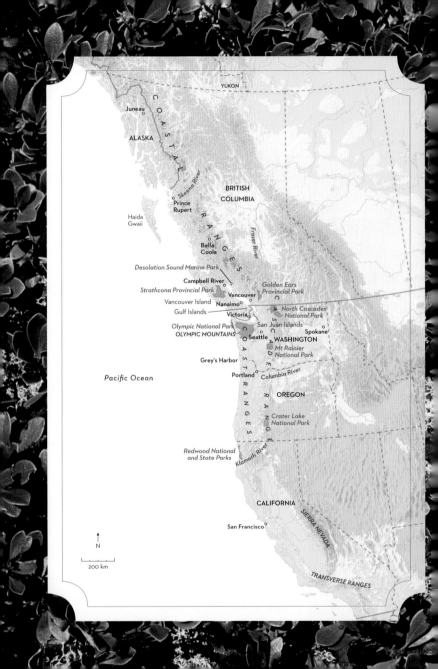

INTERCONNECTEDNESS WITH NATURE

AS A SK̲W̲X̲WÚ7MESH ETHNOBOTANIST AND TEACHER, I would love for people from all walks of life to get to know the indigenous plant species of the Pacific Northwest. My teachings are that plants have a language; they are incredible intelligent and intuitive. Through their colours, shapes, textures, and the ecosystems in which they grow, plants can help us to learn and remember what they are used for or how they work. I encourage people to observe the indigenous plant species and try to notice what pollinators they attract, which plants love to grow amongst one another, and and how do they grow through all the changes of seasons. In Sk̲w̲x̲wú7mesh snichim, the Sqaumish language, many of the moons (months) are centred on our observations of plant life. We see the months of April and May revolving around the salmon berry, and the month of August about the salal berry.

When you read about these keystone flora species, take into consideration the relationship that they have with the ecosystem. Just as we humans are part of communities, flora species are a part of a community: the forest and areas in which they grow. One of our most invaluable plants, the tree of life, the western red cedar is a plant that we give thanks to for everything we use it for: from canoes, long houses, baby cradles, and swings to weavings for baskets, clothing, food preparation and storage. The western red cedar is not only incredibly special for us as humans, but is also very sacred for animals. Wild salmon are an incredible source of fertilizer for the forests. In fact, the rings on a cedar tree can indicate the strength of the salmon run, with thicker layers of the trunk showing a strong year of salmon. The salmon nourish many species of animals from eagles, bears, wolves and, of course, people as well. Salmon and the western red cedar, the tree of life, are among the absolute most important species in the Pacific Northwest. Take these considerations into mind: each species is connected to one another, and we as people are just a small piece of the ecosystem as well. Rather than owning or controlling it, we should remember that we are just a small piece of the big puzzle.

Seńákw, Senaqwila Wyss
Skwxwú7mesh Ethnobotanist

INTRODUCTION

THIS BOOK PRESENTS fifty keystone species of flora (or rather, forty-nine flora and one fungus), some common, some less common, and all native to the coastal Pacific Northwest. It is not exhaustive by any means but is meant purely as a survey of some important species and aspires to illustrate the roles they play in the ecosystem of the PNW. The choice of plants in this book was a difficult one as the thousands of different species of terrestrial and marine plants in the PNW all play important roles in maintaining a healthy ecosystem. The species discussed in this book are a small sample of what the keen observer can discover in our forests and seaside.

A broader, more in-depth approach to flora of the region can be found in *The Flora and Fauna of Coastal British Columbia and the Pacific Northwest* (2021), as well as *The Edible and Medicinal Flora of the West Coast* (2023) and *Invasive Flora of the West Coast* (2022), to which this book can be seen as a companion of sorts. A second book presenting fifty keystone fauna species of the PNW is also available.

The species in this book have been sorted into five loose, overlapping categories, namely, flowering plants, fruit-bearing plants, fungi, marine plants, and trees and shrubs. **The species in each section have been listed alphabetically under broader categories based on their families or sub-families, such as dogwoods, brambles, or willows, which are noted on the left edge of each species profile**. An index beginning on page 122 lists not only primary common names, but the alternative common names associated with each species.

The photographs in this book were taken by myself as I explored the coastal region over a period of several years. Written with the average observer in mind, the book has an intentional bias towards plants and fungi that are visible to the typical viewer rather than more obscure species. However, it is also designed to be a quick, useful resource for readers of all levels of expertise.

For the purposes of this book, the Pacific Northwest is defined as the region stretching from Juneau, Alaska, to San Francisco, California, from the mainland coast to approximately 100 kilometres (60 miles) inland, as well as the various coastal islands.

Despite the Pacific Northwest being a very large and diverse region, the species within it are relatively uniform. Yet venture another 50 kilometres (30 miles) inland, and the ecosystem is vastly different. The species covered by this book are the delights that the ambler encounters, from the intertidal to the subalpine areas.

What is a Keystone Species?

The topmost stone in an arch is known as the keystone; it is the last stone set in place by the mason, and if it is removed, the entire arch collapses. Like an arch supported by the carefully counterbalanced forces of its stones, an ecosystem is supported by the complex interaction of the species comprising it. The loss of one species will often ripple across an entire ecosystem, sometimes with unforeseen consequences.

In the PNW perhaps no better illustration of the importance of keystone species exists than that of the sea otter (*Enhydra lutris*). The fur of the sea otter is the densest of any mammal on Earth; it is thick, warm, and naturally waterproof, and starting in the late eighteenth century it nearly doomed the species into extinction. So highly prized was the fur of the sea otter that, over the course of 160 years, *E. lutris* was all but extirpated through hunting, its population dropping to a perilous one or two thousand individuals from a peak population perhaps as high as 300,000.

The decline of the sea otter population meant a corresponding boom in the sea urchin population, for sea otters were a key urchin predator. The unchecked urchin population proceeded to lay to waste vast sections of kelp forests. Without kelp forests, thousands of species of invertebrates, mammals, fish, and birds lost a food source, shelter, and habitat. This left the entire food chain and ecosystem in disarray. Kelp forests absorb carbon dioxide from seawater and the atmosphere. They also help buffer waves, preventing coastal erosion, and help keep pollutants from reaching the shore. Only a worldwide ban on the hunting of sea otters plus extensive conservation and reintroduction efforts have brought the sea otter population back from the brink.

It is also worth understanding that a keystone is shaped to complete a *specific* arch in the same way that a key is cut to a specific lock. Ecologically speaking, a keystone species evolved in one ecosystem will rarely fulfill the same role if introduced into another. Nature does not work that way. European rabbits in Britain are considered a keystone species. They are a good source of food and beneficial in ground disturbing by burrowing warrens, grazing, and recycling nutrients in their scat. In the 1850s, Australia introduced European rabbits into their landscape to be hunted for sport. With no natural predators, the rabbit population exploded to over 600 million by 1940. Even with using biological controls, it is estimated Australia still has 200 million feral rabbits. Their entire ecosystem has been altered for the worse.

The final and perhaps most important takeaway from the keystone analogy, however, is this: While it's true that the removal of the keystone means the collapse of the arch, the larger truth is that the removal of any stone from an arch will compromise its integrity leaving it more susceptible to collapse. The same is true for an ecosystem, the architecture of which represents a profoundly complex dance of evolution and adaptation and from which the removal of any species represents a potential threat to the whole.

GLOSSARY

ANTHER	The pollen-bearing (top) portion of the stamen
AXIL	The angle made between a stalk and the stem on which it is growing
BIENNIAL	A plant that completes its life cycle in two growing seasons
BRACT	A modified leaf below the flower
CATKIN	A spike-like or drooping flower cluster, either male or female, found in species such as cottonwood
CONIFEROUS	Having evergreen leaves, usually needle-like or scaled
CORM	A swollen underground stem capable of producing roots, leaves, and flowers
DECIDUOUS	Having parts (leaves, bark) that shed annually, usually in the autumn
DIOECIOUS	Having male and female flowers on separate plants
EPIPHYTE	A plant that grows on another plant for physical support without robbing the host of nutrients

HERBACEOUS	A non-woody plant that dies back into the ground every year
HOLDFAST	A hard root-like structure used by seaweeds to attach themselves to rocks and the ocean floor
PANICLE	A branched inflorescence
PERENNIAL	General term for a plant that lives above the ground throughout the year
RHIZOME	An underground modified stem
RIPARIAN	The area along the sides of creeks, ponds, and waterways where plants grow
SEPAL	The outer parts of a flower; usually green
STIPE	A stem or stalk, such as on a mushroom, bull kelp, or the maidenhair fern
STOMATA	The pores in the epidermis of leaves; usually white
STYLE	The stem of the pistil (female organ)

FLOWERING
PLANTS

COW PARSNIP
Indian Celery
Heracleum lanatum

CARROT FAMILY Apiaceae

ECOLOGICAL ROLE Cow parsnips are one of the biggest herbaceous perennials in the PNW. With their prodigious size comes lots of annual green manure to enrich the surrounding soil. When cow parsnips colonize a burn site, their strong roots help prevent soil erosion while their large leaves deflect hard rain from directly hitting the ground. The plants are an important browse for elk, deer, bears, grouse, pheasants, waterfowl, and smaller rodents.

DESCRIPTION Cow parsnip is a tall, hollow-stemmed, herbaceous perennial 1–3 m (3.3–10 ft.) high. Its small white flowers are grouped in flat-topped, umbrella-like terminal clusters to 25 cm (10 in.) across. It produces numerous small, egg-shaped seeds, 1 cm (0.5 in.) long, with a pleasant aroma. The large woolly compound leaves are divided into three leaflets, one terminal and two lateral, to 30 cm (12 in.) across.

ETYMOLOGY The genus name *Heracleum* is fitting for this plant of Herculean proportions.

HABITAT Moist forests, meadows, marshes, and roadsides from low to high elevations.

CAUTION Cow parsnip can cause severe blistering and rashes when handled.

CATTAIL
Broadleaf Cattail / Bulrush
Typha latifolia

CATTAIL FAMILY Typhaceae

ECOLOGICAL ROLE Cattails occupy the ecological wetland area between the terrestrial zone and the aquatic zone. This semi-aquatic zone is an extremely important transition habitat that supplies shelter, food, and nesting sites and materials for wetland birds, mammals, amphibians, insects, waterfowl, reptiles, and plants. Marsh wrens and yellow-headed and red-winged blackbirds all perch and build their nests on and in cattail marshes. Canada geese, muskrats, beavers, fish, raccoons, and deer use these areas as a food source and shelter. Salamanders, frogs, and dragonflies lay their eggs in the water between them and on them. As these eggs hatch, they themselves become a food source for land and freshwater fish, birds, and animals.

DESCRIPTION Cattails are semi-aquatic perennials that can grow to 2.5 m (8 ft.) in height. The distinctive "tail," a brown spike, is 15–20 cm (6–8 in.) long, 3 cm (1 in.) wide, and made up of male and female flowers. The lighter-coloured male flowers grow at the top and usually fall off, leaving a bare spike above the familiar brown female flowers. The sword-shaped leaves are alternate and spongy at the base.

ETYMOLOGY The species name *latifolia* means "broad leaved."

HABITAT Common at low to mid elevations, at lakesides and riversides, and in ponds, marshes, and ditches.

BUNCHBERRY
Dwarf Dogwood
Cornus canadensis

DOGWOOD FAMILY Cornaceae

ECOLOGICAL ROLE Bunchberry's fruit is an important food source for black bears, hares, rabbits, martens, squirrels, grouse, songbirds, and migratory birds. Bunchberry has a habit of flowering twice, once in the spring and then again in the late summer. The twigs and leaves are an excellent low-ground, year-round browse for elk, deer, and interior caribou. It is an interesting situation being in a completely silent elevated bog and suddenly hearing a buzzing sound that gets louder and louder, then finding the source is hundreds of bumblebees pollinating the bunchberry flowers.

DESCRIPTION Bunchberry is a perennial no higher than 20 cm (8 in.) tall. The tiny greenish flowers are surrounded by four showy white bracts, just like the flowers of the larger dogwood. The evergreen leaves, 4–7 cm (2–3 in.) long, grow in whorls of five to seven and have parallel veins like the larger tree. The beautiful red berries form in bunches (hence the name) just above the leaves in August.

ETYMOLOGY The species name *canadensis* refers to Canada, although it is also native to China, Japan, Eastern Russia, Greenland, United States, and Korea.

HABITAT From low to high elevations in cool, moist coniferous forests and bogs.

RED-OSIER DOGWOOD
Cornus stolonifera

DOGWOOD FAMILY Cornaceae

ECOLOGICAL ROLE The upper branch structure of the red-osier dog-woods is very suitable for nesting songbirds, while the tight bottom branch pattern protects amphibians and small mammals. The leaves and twigs provide summer through winter browse for deer, moose, mountain goats, bighorn sheep, beavers, and rabbits. Starting in late May, the flowers are a source of nectar and pollen for butterflies and moths, while the fruit (drupes) that ripen by end of July are high in fat and are a nutritious source of food for waxwings, band-tailed pigeons, northern flickers, and bears.

DESCRIPTION Red-osier dogwood is a mid-sized deciduous shrub to 5 m (16 ft.) in height. Its small white flowers—0.7 cm (0.25 in.) across—are grouped together to form dense round clusters approximately 10 cm (4 in.) across. The leaves are typical of dogwood: opposite and to 10 cm (4 in.) long, with parallel veins. Younger branches are pliable and have an attractive red colour.

ETYMOLOGY The common name red-osier refers to the tough red branches, which are used in wickerwork, basketry, and woven fencing.

HABITAT Moist to wet areas, usually forested, at low to mid elevations.

FIREWEED
Epilobium angustifolium

EVENING PRIMROSE FAMILY Onagraceae

ECOLOGICAL ROLE Fireweed is one of the first plants to return to sites that have been burned off, logged, suffered an avalanche, or disturbed. As a fibrous rooted herbaceous perennial, fireweed's roots hold the soil together, which prevents erosion; the stalks and leaves above ground supply annual green manure. The flowers have copious amounts of nectar, which attracts honeybees, bumblebees, moths, and butterflies. A single fireweed plant can produce up to 80,000 seeds annually, which, with their cotton-like parachutes, can repopulate a vacant site in a very short period. As the forest service says, where there is fireweed, there is wildlife: bears, deer, elk, rabbits, and muskrats feed on the leaves and new shoots. The plants are also larval hosts to several species of moths and butterflies.

DESCRIPTION Fireweed is a tall herbaceous perennial that reaches heights of 3 m (10 ft.) in good soil. Its purple-red flowers grow on long, showy terminal clusters. The leaves are alternate, lance shaped like a willow's, about 10–20 cm (4–8 in.) long, and darker green above than below. The minute seeds are produced in pods 5–10 cm (2–4 in.) long and have silky hairs for easy wind dispersal. Fireweed flowers have long been a beekeeper's favourite.

ETYMOLOGY The common name fireweed comes from the fact that it is one of the first plants to grow on burned sites; it typically follows wildfires.

HABITAT Common throughout BC in open areas and at burned sites.

CANADA GOLDENROD
Solidago canadensis

ASTER FAMILY Asteraceae

ECOLOGICAL ROLE Goldenrods are considered top-ranked herbaceous plants for biodiversity—their flowers attract bees, flies, beetles, moths, and butterflies, which in turn attract preying birds, spiders, and beetles. Their late summer/fall blooming provides much-needed pollen and nectar for honeybees, bumblebees, and monarch butterflies. This ensures bees will have enough honey for winter. Goldenrod flowers are insect pollinated; their pollen/nectar is heavy and sticky, which means it cannot be picked up by the wind. A bonus for people who suffer from hay-fever.

DESCRIPTION Canada goldenrod is a herbaceous perennial of various heights, from 0.3 m (1 ft.) to 1.5 m (5 ft.). Its small golden flowers are densely packed to form terminal pyramidal clusters. The many small leaves grow at the base of the flowers; they are alternate, lance linear, and sharply saw-toothed to smooth.

ETYMOLOGY The genus name *Solidago* is Latin for "to make whole or strengthen," referring to its medicinal properties.

HABITAT Roadsides, wastelands, and forest edges at low to mid elevations.

ORANGE HONEYSUCKLE
Climbing Honeysuckle / Western Trumpet Honeysuckle
Lonicera ciliosa

HONEYSUCKLE FAMILY Caprifoliaceae

ECOLOGICAL ROLE The long throats on the flowers of native honeysuckles such as purple and orange honeysuckle seem to be made exclusively for hummingbirds; however, moths, butterflies, and bees seem fine extracting the pollen and nectar. Crawling insects that enter and exit the flowers not only play an important role in pollinating but also in attracting insectivorous insects, which in turn attract birds. Though poisonous to humans, the red berries that ripen by summer's end cause a commotion among the feeding waxwings, flickers, robins, jays, thrushes, finches, grouse, ring-necked pheasants, and grosbeaks.

DESCRIPTION Orange honeysuckle is a deciduous woody vine capable of climbing trees to 8 m (26 ft.) in height. Its orange flowers are trumpet shaped, to 4 cm (1.5 in.) long, and form in clusters in the terminal leaves. By late summer, bunches of bright-red berries are produced in the cup-shaped leaves. The leaves are oval, 5–8 cm (2–3 in.) long, and, like all honeysuckles, opposite. This species is the showiest of the native honeysuckles. Its main pollinators are hummingbirds and moths.

ETYMOLOGY The genus name *Lonicera* commemorates Adam Lonitzer (1528–1586) a German naturalist. The species name *ciliosa* means "having hair like eyelashes," which refers to the hairy leaf edges.

HABITAT Scattered in low-elevation Douglas fir forests, but more common near the ocean.

There are dozens of honeysuckle species in the coastal PNW, including pink honeysuckle (*L. hispidula*), twinberry honeysuckle (*L. involucrata*), and climbing honeysuckle

WESTERN PINK FAWN LILY
Coast Fawn Lily
Erythronium revolutum

LILY FAMILY Liliaceae

ECOLOGICAL ROLE Fawn lilies are considered important woodland plants because their large colonies act as soil stabilizers for the forest floor. Their short emergence from March to April means they leave a lot of nutrients and green compost when they die back. The flowers are pollinated by bumblebees, Anna's hummingbirds, moths, and butterflies. The early emerging leaves are an excellent browse for black-tailed and mule deer.

DESCRIPTION Western pink fawn lily is a herbaceous perennial to 30 cm (12 in.) in height. The nodding pink flowers are adorned with golden anthers. The seed takes five to seven years to form a corm and put up its first flower. The leaves are basal, lance shaped, to 20 cm (8 in.) long, and mottled white to dark green.

ETYMOLOGY The genus name *Erythronium* is from the Greek *erythros* [red], probably referring to the pink flowers on some species.

HABITAT Open forests at low elevations, usually in sandy soil by rivers and streams. The picking of the flowers by people has greatly reduced the numbers of this plant.

The lilies of the PNW include the tiger lily (*L. columbianum*), western white fawn lily (*E. oregonum*), yellow glacier lily (*E. grandiflorum*), and western pink fawn lily.

LARGE-LEAVED LUPINE
Lupinus polyphyllus

PEA FAMILY Fabaceae

ECOLOGICAL ROLE Lupines are a member of the pea family that takes atmospheric nitrogen and fixes it into its roots and surrounding soil. The lupine genus is considered a pioneer species. It quickly reclaims disturbed sites, avalanche tracks, gravelly slopes, and stream banks, and helps with soil fertility, erosion control, and bringing back wildlife. Its flower (June to July) attracts honeybees, bumblebees, and hummingbirds.

DESCRIPTION The large-leaved lupine and its cultivars are the lupines you are most likely to see in parks and gardens. In its natural setting, the large-leaved lupine grows to 1.5 m (5 ft.) in height. The blue pea-like flowers are borne in clusters to 40 cm (16 in.) long. The large leaves consist of 10 to 17 leaflets, up to 12 cm (5 in.) long. The seeds are in hairy pods to 5 cm (2 in.) long.

ETYMOLOGY The species name *polyphyllus* means "with many leaves."

HABITAT Moist sunny areas from sea level to mid elevations.

The PNW is home to dozens of species of lupine including the Arctic lupine (*L. arcticus*), Nootka lupine (*L. nootkatensis*), and the large-leaved lupine.

WILD MINT
Field Mint / Corn Mint
Mentha arvensis

MINT FAMILY Lamiaceae

ECOLOGICAL ROLE When in flower (April/May to September/October), wild mint is extremely important to honeybees, bumblebees, moths, and butterflies. Wild patches of mint will flower throughout most of the summer, providing a reliable annual source of nectar. The fragrant leaves are a food source for slugs, snails, cut worms, leaf hoppers, aphids, mint leaf beetle, and mites, which in turn are food for larger forest animals.

DESCRIPTION Wild mint is an aromatic, square-stemmed herbaceous perennial 15–60 cm (6–24 in.) in height. The grass-green leaves sit opposite in pairs, are fuzzy, serrated, and to 6.5 cm (2.5 in.) long. The flowers are borne in whorls at the leaf bases and range from dirty white to pink to pale purple.

ETYMOLOGY The genus name *Mentha* is from the name of the Greek nymph Minthe, the mistress of Hades, who is the ruler of the underworld. When his queen, Persephone, found out about Minthe, she had her trampled to the ground and turned into a plant. In response, Hades made sure that the more the plant was trampled the sweeter it would smell. The species name *arvensis* means "from the fields."

HABITAT Wild mint grows in moist fields and forest edges. I have found several wild patches from which I harvest four to five kilograms a year.

STINGING NETTLE
Urtica dioica

NETTLE FAMILY Urticaceae

ECOLOGICAL ROLE Finding a patch of stinging nettles is a good indicator of nitrogen-rich soil and that alders or bigleaf maples are or were nearby. Stinging nettles fix atmospheric nitrogen into their leaves and roots, which feeds the soil nitrogen and a compost layer through herbaceous die-back over many seasons. Stinging nettles start to flower the beginning of May and are first-rate wildlife attractors of butterflies, including tortoiseshells, red admirals, and commas whose larvae feast on the leaves. Ladybirds enjoy consuming the aphids, which in turn invite woodland birds and amphibians.

DESCRIPTION Stinging nettle is a herbaceous perennial to over 2 m (6.6 ft.) high. Its tiny flowers are greenish and produced in hanging clusters to 5 cm (2 in.) long. The leaves are heart-shaped at the base, tapered at the top, coarsely toothed, and to 10 cm (4 in.) long. The stalks, stems, and leaves all have stinging hairs that contain formic acid. Many people have the misfortune of encountering this plant the hard way.

ETYMOLOGY The genus name *Urtica* is from the Latin *uro* [to burn].

HABITAT Thrives in moist, nutrient-rich, somewhat shady disturbed sites, where it can form great masses. Stinging nettles are usually an indicator of nitrogen-rich soil.

CAUTION As mentioned above, almost the entire plant is covered in tiny hairs containing formic acid, which causes a stinging sensation and rash when touched. Take precautions by wearing protective clothing and avoid touching the plant directly.

FAIRYSLIPPER
Calypso Orchid
Calypso bulbosa

ORCHID FAMILY Orchidaceae

ECOLOGICAL ROLE The spring flowering of fairyslippers coincides with the emergence of new queen bumblebees. The early flowers are not a great source of pollen for the queen, but enough to help start up her new colony. Fairyslipper orchids are an indication that the environment around them is healthy. The plants do not tolerate habitat destruction—logging, encroachment of invasive species, picking, or pollution. The claim that fairyslippers are persnickety and that's why they are rare is not quite true. They prosper by just being left alone, much like most people. If you do find a patch of fairyslippers, you are in a healthy environment. Take a minute and enjoy the fresh air.

DESCRIPTION The fairyslipper is a delicate herbaceous perennial with corms to 20 cm (8 in.) in height. Its flower is light purple; the lower lip is lighter and decorated with spots, stripes, and coloured hairs. The single leaf is broadly lanceolate and withers with the flower; a new leaf appears in late summer and remains through the winter. This is one of the most beautiful of the Pacific Northwest's native orchids.

ETYMOLOGY The genus name *Calypso* comes to us from Greek mythology where Calypso is the sea nymph who detained Odysseus on the island of Ogygia for seven years.

HABITAT Mostly associated with Douglas fir and grand fir forests.

CAUTION Fairyslipper, and other orchids, are considered endangered species and should not be disturbed or removed from where they are growing. It is illegal in BC to relocate orchids from their native environment.

WESTERN SPRING BEAUTY
Claytonia lanceolata

PURSLANE FAMILY Montiaceae

ECOLOGICAL ROLE The great abundance of western spring beauty growing on alpine to mid-alpine slopes and valleys helps to control soil erosion in avalanche prone areas. The flowers and leaves are a spring–summer browse for elk, deer, rabbits, and hares. The corms are sought after by black and grizzly bears, squirrels, and ground squirrels. The early emerging flowers are equipped with nectar guides much like running lights directing bees and other pollinating insects to the nectar glands. Western spring beauty is very generous with its nectar production. This in turn feeds the native bee populations and guarantees pollination.

DESCRIPTION Western spring beauty is a herbaceous perennial from a marble-sized corm to 10–20 cm (4–8 in.) tall. The beautiful white to pink flowers have five petals, with darker-pink veins.

ETYMOLOGY The genus name *Claytonia* commemorates John Clayton (1686–1773). Clayton has been described as one of the greatest botanists in America. He corresponded with some of the greats of the day: George Washington, Thomas Jefferson, Carl Linnaeus, and John Bartram.

HABITAT Mid to high elevations; usually seen chasing the snowpack as it melts.

BALDHIP ROSE
Woodland Rose
Rosa gymnocarpa

ROSE FAMILY Rosaceae

ECOLOGICAL ROLE All three of the common native roses mentioned below grow in natural thickets and provide shelter and nesting sites for birds and small mammals. The June flowers are aesthetically a bonus for humans but are meant for pollinating insects, bees, butterflies, and birds. The ripe pips/hips or haws are a food source for waxwings, blackbirds, thrushes, rabbits, squirrels, and bears, which in turn disperse the seeds with a dollop of manure.

DESCRIPTION The baldhip rose is the Pacific Northwest's smallest native rose. It is often prostrate to 1.5 m (5 ft.) in height. The tiny pink flowers are five petalled, delicately fragrant, 1–2 cm (0.5–1 in.) across, and usually solitary. The compound leaves are smaller than those of the Nootka rose (*R. nutkana*) and have five to nine toothed leaflets. The spindly stems are mostly armed, with weak prickles. A good identifier is this rose's unusual habit of losing its sepals, leaving the hip bald.

ETYMOLOGY The species name *gymnocarpa* means "naked fruit."

HABITAT Dry open forests at lower elevations, from southern BC to the redwood forests of California.

There are close to two dozen species of roses native to the PNW, including Nootka rose (*R. nutkana*), swamp rose (*R. pisocarpa*), and baldhip rose.

EDIBLE THISTLE
Cirsium edule

ASTER FAMILY Asteraceae

ECOLOGICAL ROLE Edible thistles are an important food species for songbirds. American goldfinches are known to coordinate the birth of their young with thistles in full seed production. Examine a songbird's nest and more often than not the thistledown can be seen in their nest construction. The flowers produce copious amounts of pollen and nectar for bees and butterflies like monarchs, swallowtails, skippers, and fritillaries.

DESCRIPTION Edible thistle is a showy biennial and sometimes perennial that can grow as tall as 2 m (6.6 ft.) in favourable conditions. The well-armed leaves are alternating and lance shaped, with spined lobes. The beautiful pinkish-purple flowers nod when young. Short-style thistle (*C. brevistylum*) is similar, except the styles are shorter.

HABITAT Lightly covered forest edges and moist meadows.

WAPATO
Arrowhead / Duck Potato
Sagittaria latifolia

WATER PLANTAIN FAMILY Alismataceae

ECOLOGICAL ROLE Wapato is a food source for beavers, porcupines, muskrats, and the occasional bear. The ripe seeds (about 20,000 per plant) are a feast for swans, geese, and ducks, while the large arrow-shaped leaves provide shelter for fish and aquatic insects.

DESCRIPTION Wapato is a herbaceous freshwater perennial that can grow to 90 cm (36 in.) tall. The arrow-shaped leaves, up to 25 cm (10 in.) long, grow on long, slightly arching stalks. The waxy white flowers are produced in whorls of three on long leafless stems.

ETYMOLOGY The common name wapato is from the Chinook, meaning "tuberous plant." When wapato leaves and small tubers can be seen floating on the water, it usually is an indication of ducks or muskrats that have dislodged the plants for their starchy tubers (hence the name "duck potato").

HABITAT Low elevations, shallow ponds, sloughs, lake edges, and slow-moving streams.

OREGON OXALIS
Redwood Sorrel
Oxalis oregana

WOODSORREL FAMILY Oxalidaceae

ECOLOGICAL ROLE These plants native to the PNW thrive in the deep shade of Douglas firs and coast redwoods, requiring very little light to effectively photosynthesize. It grows well in a compost layer of leaves, conifer needles, twigs, and rotting branches and spreads rhizomatically across the forest floor. It shows off its white-pink flowers starting in April, attracting native bees, butterflies, and syrphid flies.

DESCRIPTION Oregon oxalis is a delicate-looking perennial to 15 cm (6 in.) tall. The white to pinkish flowers are borne singly on slender stalks that are shorter than the leaves. The shamrock-like leaves have three heart-shaped leaflets to 15 cm (6 in.) tall. Both the flower and leaf stalks arise from the plant base.

ETYMOLOGY The genus name *Oxalis* means "acid," "sour," or "sharp," in reference to the taste of the leaves.

HABITAT Moist forested areas at low to mid elevations.

CAUTION Although the leaves are edible, they contain oxalic acid and should only be consumed very sparingly or avoided completely.

FRUIT-BEARING PLANTS

PACIFIC CRAB APPLE
Malus fusca

ROSE FAMILY Rosaceae

ECOLOGICAL ROLE Pacific crab apple is the only native apple in the PNW, which puts high demands on the small sweet and sour fruit from grouse, robins, jays, waxwings, squirrels, mice, chipmunks, raccoons, and black bears, who are known to rip the branches off to access the apples. The leaves and branch tips are excellent browse for elk and deer.

DESCRIPTION Pacific crab apple is a deciduous shrub or small tree about 2–10 m (6.6–33 ft.) in height. Its leaves are 5–10 cm (2–4 in.) long and similar to those of orchard apple trees, except that they often have bottom lobes. The flowers are typical apple blossoms: white to pink, fragrant, and in clusters of 5 to 12. The fruit that follows is 1–2 cm (0.5–1 in.) across and green at first, turning yellowy reddish. On older trees, the bark is scaly and deeply fissured.

HABITAT High beaches, moist open forests, swamps, and stream banks at lower elevations.

KINNIKINNICK
Bearberry
Arctostaphylos uva-ursi

HEATHER FAMILY Ericaceae

ECOLOGICAL ROLE Kinnikinnick berries, from June to September, are also a favourite for mountain sheep, grouse, bears, moose, songbirds, wild turkeys, and in the Arctic, polar bears. The spring flowers attract honeybees and bumblebees, while the leaves are larval hosts to fourteen species of moths and butterflies. Deer and rabbits will browse the foliage in the winter, keeping the plants compact and more useful for soil stabilization.

DESCRIPTION Kinnikinnick is a trailing, mat-forming evergreen that rarely grows above 25 cm (10 in.) in height. Its fragrant pinkish flowers bloom in spring and are replaced by bright-red berries 1 cm (0.5 in.) across by late summer. The small oval leaves grow to 3 cm (1 in.) long and are leathery and alternate.

ETYMOLOGY Kinnikinnick is an Ojibwe word used to describe a tobacco mix.

HABITAT Dry rock outcrops and well-drained forest areas from sea level to high elevations.

BOG BLUEBERRY
Bog Bilberry
Vaccinium uliginosum

HEATHER FAMILY Ericaceae

ECOLOGICAL ROLE Blueberries provide an essential and pleasant meal for hundreds of birds, mammals, and insects. Berries are ripe by July, and black bear populations will fluctuate according to how productive the blueberry crops are in certain years. The entire bush could be considered a wildlife corner store—the flowers attract many pollinators, especially bees; the leaves and twigs are a summer to winter browse for deer, elk, bears, skunks, and rabbits; and the berries have an endless guestlist.

DESCRIPTION Bog blueberry is a small deciduous bush to 60 cm (24 in.) in height. At high elevations, it may reach only 10 cm (4 in.) in height. The tiny pink flowers give way to dark-blue berries that have a waxy coating. The berries are delicious. The leaves are green above and pale on the underside, to 3 cm (1 in.) long, with no teeth.

ETYMOLOGY The species name *uliginosum* means "of the marsh/swamp/bog."

HABITAT Low elevated bogs along the coast to subalpine scrub.

Blueberries of the PNW include the oval-leaved blueberry (*V. ovalifolium*), the dwarf blueberry (*V. cespitosum*), and the bog blueberry.

BLACK RASPBERRY
Blackcap
Rubus leucodermis

ROSE FAMILY Rosaceae

ECOLOGICAL ROLE Black raspberries are not true berries. They are many tiny individual fruits called drupelets that coalesce and form a large fruit with many bumps. The advantage of this merger of tiny drupelets is that the mature fruit is filled with naturally sweetened juice, making them irresistible to herbivores and omnivores in the PNW. Like other *Rubus* species, it provides food for many species and nectar for countless pollinators. The berries ripen from July to August, depending on elevation.

DESCRIPTION Black raspberry is an armed deciduous shrub to 2 m (6.6 ft.) in height. Its white flowers are small, to 3 cm (1 in.) across, and borne in terminal clusters of three to seven. The resulting fruit to 1 cm (0.5 in.) across starts off red but turns dark purple to black by July or August. The leaves have three to five leaflets supported on long, arching, well-armed stems. Black raspberries can be distinguished from other raspberries by the bloom, a whitish waxy coating, on the stems.

HABITAT Open forests and forest edges at low to mid elevations.

SALMONBERRY
Rubus spectabilis

ROSE FAMILY Rosaceae

ECOLOGICAL ROLE Like other *Rubus* species, the salmonberry is not a true berry but rather an aggregate fruit of juicy drupelets. The spring flowering salmonberry is an important provider of early nectar for pollinating insects. The fruit, from mid-June to mid-July, is eaten by birds and mammals alike, and its leaves and twigs are browsed by deer, elk, and other herbivores. Salmonberry is often a fire survivor and plays a role in the early regeneration of burnt-out areas.

DESCRIPTION Salmonberry is one of BC's tallest native berry bushes. Though it averages 2–3 m (6.6–10 ft.) in height, the bush can grow up to 4 m (13 ft.) high. The bell-shaped pink flowers are 4 cm (1.5 in.) across; they bloom at the end of February and are a welcome sight. Flowering continues until June, when both the flowers and the ripe fruit can be seen on the same bush. The soft berries range in colour from yellow to orange to red, with the occasional dark purple, and are shaped like blackberries. The leaves are compound, with three leaflets, much like the leaves of a raspberry. Weak prickles may be seen on the lower portion of the branches; the tops are unarmed.

ETYMOLOGY The berry's common name comes from its resemblance to the shape and colour of salmon eggs.

HABITAT Common on the coast in shaded damp forests.

THIMBLEBERRY
Rubus parviflorus

ROSE FAMILY Rosaceae

ECOLOGICAL ROLE Another species of the *Rubus* genus like blackberries, raspberries, and salmonberries whose sweet aggregate fruit, from July to early August, feeds all manner of birds and mammals, whose flowers provide nectar for pollinators, and whose shoots and twigs serve as browse for herbivores.

DESCRIPTION Thimbleberry is an unarmed shrub to 3 m (10 ft.) in height. Its large white flowers open up to 5 cm (2 in.) across and are replaced by juicy bright-red berries. The dome-shaped berries are 2 cm (1 in.) across and bear little resemblance to a thimble, until they're picked. The maple-shaped leaves grow up to 25 cm (10 in.) across.

ETYMOLOGY When the ripe berries are picked, the central core is left behind, giving the berry in hand the appearance of a sewing thimble.

HABITAT Common in coastal forests at low to mid elevations.

TRAILING BLACKBERRY
Rubus ursinus

ROSE FAMILY Rosaceae

ECOLOGICAL ROLE Like raspberries, the trailing blackberry is an aggregate fruit made up of succulent drupelets. During the fruiting season, starting mid-July, there is a lineup of deer, elk, bears, coyotes, raccoons, skunks, rodents, robins, cardinals, bluebirds, jays, and varied thrushes gorging on the fruit and then dispersing the seeds. In early spring, most species of *Rubus* push up suckers around their bases. These suckers are a vital food source after a long hard winter for elk, deer, bears, and hares.

DESCRIPTION Trailing blackberry is a moderately armed vine to 5 m (16 ft.) across. The berries are smaller than the introduced varieties, but I find them sweeter, and they ripen earlier.

ETYMOLOGY The species name *ursinus* comes from the Latin *ursa* [bear] probably referring to bears enjoying these berries.

HABITAT The trailing blackberry, which is native to the Pacific Northwest, can tolerate more shade than the introduced species. It can usually be seen at the forest edge.

The four most common blackberries of the PNW are the cutleaf (*R. laciniatus*), Himalayan (*R. bifrons*), Armenian (*R. armeniacus*), and trailing blackberries. Of these four, only the lattermost is a native species.

CROWBERRY
Empetrum nigrum

CROWBERRY FAMILY Empetraceae

ECOLOGICAL ROLE In early winter when there is snow on the ground, the berries and twigs become a vital source of food for deer, elk, rabbits, and hares. You will often see ungulates hoofing snow away to access the plants. Black bears are usually taking it easy at this time of year. By this time, the berries, which ripen from August to October, are loaded with much-needed sugars, some of which may have fermented into intoxicating alcohol. The plants can flower as late as June, supplying much-needed nectar to mid-altitude bees and other pollinating insects.

DESCRIPTION Crowberry is a low heather-like shrub to 30 cm (12 in.) in height. The small purplish flowers are borne two to three in the leaf axils. The plants are mostly dioecious, with male and female flowers on separate plants. The crow-black berries are to 1 cm (0.5 in.) across.

ETYMOLOGY The genus name *Empetrum* is from the Greek *enpetros* [on a rock], referring to where it prefers to grow.

HABITAT Bogs and bluffs along the coast.

RED-FLOWERING CURRANT

Ribes sanguineum

CURRANT AND GOOSEBERRY FAMILY Grossulariaceae

ECOLOGICAL ROLE Currants are extremely hardy and can be the last of the fruiting bushes as you hike into the alpine slopes. They are an important food source for both black and grizzly bears as they can be one of the last berry species they will consume before hibernating. Also, at mid to high elevations, the bushes offer cover, nesting, and food for birds and small animals—ptarmigan, grouse, quail, rabbits, hares, squirrels—which in turn are a food source for golden eagles. The larvae of various moths and butterflies depend on currant leaves. At mid to high elevations, when the bushes are in full bloom, the flowers attract pollinating insects. The berries that follow the flowers are not overly sweet; however, they do attract the usual crowd of omnivores and herbivores.

DESCRIPTION Red-flowering currant is an upright deciduous bush 1.5–3 m (5–10 ft.) in height. Its flowers range in colour from pale pink to bright crimson and hang in 8–12 cm (3–5 in.) panicles. The bluish-black berries, 1 cm (0.5 in.) across, are inviting to eat but are usually dry and bland. The leaves are 5–10 cm (2–4 in.) across and maple shaped, with three to five lobes.

ETYMOLOGY The species name *sanguineum* refers to the colour of the flowers.

HABITAT Dry open forests at low to mid elevations.

The PNW boasts more than a dozen species of currants including the stink currant (*R. bracteosum*), swamp currant (*R. lacustre*), and red-flowering currant.

BLUE-BERRIED ELDER
Blue Elderberry
Sambucus caerulea

MOSCHATEL FAMILY Adoxaceae

ECOLOGICAL ROLE Elders are an ecological niche all by themselves. The pollen laden flowers attract most species of local bees, wasps, flies, moths, butterflies, and crawling insects. The fruit, when ripe, attract a cacophony of sounds from all the different feeding songbirds. If any berries are left behind, black bears will happily finish them off. I have seen coyotes chase birds out of the bushes, bend the branches down and eat the berries, which can last into October. The leaves and twigs are a food source for a variety of moth larvae, elk, and deer. The high angles of the branch unions make sturdy platforms for bird nest construction. The hollow stems provide a home to mason bees and even a magic wand for Albus Dumbledore (*Harry Potter*).

DESCRIPTION Blue-berried elder ranges in size from a bush to a small tree about 6 m (20 ft.) tall. Its flowers are similar to those of the red-berried elder but are in flat-topped clusters, not pyramidal. The mature berries are dark blue with a white coating of the bloom, giving them a soft-blue appearance. The leaves are compound, with five to nine oval, lance-shaped leaflets.

HABITAT Dry open sites at low elevations. The blue-berried elder is found in inland areas and the Gulf Islands and San Juan Islands.

There are two species of elder native to the PNW, the red-berried elder (*S. racemose*) and the blue-berried elder.

SALAL
Gaultheria shallon

HEATHER FAMILY Ericaceae

ECOLOGICAL ROLE Salal is a food and nectar source for hundreds of mammals, birds, and insects. The leaves are an integral part of the diets of elk, black-tailed and mule deer, and mountain beavers. Also, the evergreen leaves provide a cool shelter and bedding for young deer and elk, birds, and smaller mammals. The berries, which ripen at the beginning of August, are enjoyed by bears, coyotes, deer, red and Douglas squirrels, chipmunks, songbirds, band-tailed pigeons, jays, woodpeckers, and grouse. The flowers are pollinated by hummingbirds, bees, wasps, moths, and flies.

DESCRIPTION Salal is a prostrate to mid-sized bush that grows to 0.5–4 m (1.7–13 ft.) in height. In spring, the small pinkish flowers to 1 cm (0.5 in.) long hang like strings of tiny Chinese lanterns. The edible dark-purple berries grow to 1 cm (0.5 in.) across and ripen by mid-August or September. Both the flowers and the berries display themselves for several weeks. The dark-green leaves are 7–10 cm (3–4 in.) long, tough, and oval shaped. Salal is often overlooked by some berry pickers, but the ripe berries taste excellent when fresh and make fine preserves and wine.

ETYMOLOGY The genus name *Gaultheria* commemorates the Canadian physician and botanist Jean-François Gaultier (1708–1758).

HABITAT Dry to moist forested areas along the entire coast.

OREGON GRAPE
Mahonia nervosa

BARBERRY FAMILY Berberidaceae

ECOLOGICAL ROLE Both *M. nervosa* and *M. aquifolium* are referenced as grapes, but only by colour and shape, not by their sugar content. The tart berries turn blue and persist through autumn, attracting a following of coyotes, bears, raccoons, cedar waxwings, Swainson's thrushes, grouses, ring-neck pheasants, juncos, towhees, and sparrows. When in flower, the bushes create a buzz with the different bees, moths, butterflies, and Anna's hummingbirds. As spiney as the leaves are, they are a browse for elk, deer, bears, and other herbivores and omnivores.

DESCRIPTION Oregon grape is a small spreading understory shrub that is very noticeable when the upright bright-yellow flowers are in bloom. By midsummer, the clusters of small green fruit, 1 cm (0.5 in.) across, turn an attractive grape-blue. The leaves are evergreen, holly-like, waxy, and compound, usually with 9 to 17 leaflets. The bark is rough, light grey outside, and brilliant yellow inside. Another species, tall Oregon grape (*M. aquifolium*), grows in a more open and dry location, is taller, growing to 2 m (6.6 ft.), and has fewer leaflets (five to nine).

ETYMOLOGY The species name *nervosa* refers to the leaves having several veins branching out from the leaf base (as opposed to a single central vein. In the tall variant, the species name *aquifolium* means "holly-like."

HABITAT Dry coniferous forests in southern coastal BC and Washington.

SASKATOON BERRY
Serviceberry
Amelanchier alnifolia

ROSE FAMILY Rosaceae

ECOLOGICAL ROLE Once established, saskatoon berries are drought resistant and excellent for soil retention in coastal or rocky areas. The early flowering in April and May provides much needed nectar and pollen for bees, butterflies, and other pollinating insects. The June fruit is quickly eaten by cedar waxwings, grouse, bluebirds, robins, cardinals, along with raccoons, foxes, deer, bears, and opossums.

DESCRIPTION Depending on growing conditions, the Saskatoon berry can vary from a 1 m (3.3 ft.) shrub to a small tree 7 m (23 ft.) in height. The white showy flowers are 1–3 cm (0.5–1.2 in.) across and often hang in pendulous clusters. The young reddish berries form early and darken to a purple-black by midsummer. The berries are up to 1 cm (0.5 in.) across. The light bluish-green leaves are deciduous, oval shaped, and toothed above the middle.

ETYMOLOGY The common name saskatoon derives from the Cree word for the berry, misâskwatômina. The city of Saskatoon, Saskatchewan, is named for the berry (not the other way around).

HABITAT Shorelines, rocky outcrops, and open forests at low to mid elevations.

OSOBERRY
Indian Plum / Oregon Plum
Oemleria cerasiformis

ROSE FAMILY Rosaceae

ECOLOGICAL ROLE Osoberry is one of the first native bushes to flower in the PNW, and with the first flowers comes the first nectar and pollen. This late-winter flowering is important to Anna's hummingbirds, native bees, moths, and butterflies. The fruit, by the end of June, though in limited quantities, is consumed by bears, deer, coyotes, waxwings, robins, and the occasional fox. Its fibrous, sucking roots make it ideal for controlling soil erosion in local riparian areas, especially in logged areas.

DESCRIPTION Osoberry is an upright deciduous shrub or small tree to 5 m (16 ft.) in height. Its white flowers, which usually emerge before the leaves, are 1 cm (0.5 in.) across and hang in clusters 6–10 cm (2–4 in.) long. The small plum-like fruit grow to 1 cm (0.5 in.) across; they start off yellowish and red and finish a bluish-black. They are edible, but a large seed and bitter taste make them better for the birds. The leaves are broadly lance shaped, light green, 7–12 cm (3–5 in.) long, and appear in upright clusters.

ETYMOLOGY The species name *cerasiformis* means "cherry shaped," a reference to the fruit.

HABITAT Restricted to low elevations on the southern coast and Gulf Islands; prefers moist open broad-leaved forests.

SQUASHBERRY
Mooseberry / Highbush Cranberry
Viburnum edule

MOSCHATEL FAMILY Adoxaceae

ECOLOGICAL ROLE Squashberries are another pioneer species that will regenerate from its roots or stump after a forest fire. The mature fruit, from September to October, is a favourite for grizzly and black bears, songbirds, and grouse, while the foliage is a browse for beavers, snowshoe hares, deer, elk, bighorn sheep, and mountain goats. The bushes are prone to heavy infestations of tent caterpillars, mites, scale, and aphids, which in turn are food for other insects and birds.

DESCRIPTION Squashberry is usually seen as a straggling bush 3 m (10 ft.) in height. Its small white flowers, to 1 cm (0.5 in.) across, are borne in rounded clusters nestled between the paired leaves. The resulting red berries, to 1.5 cm (0.5 in.) across, grow in clusters of two to five. The leaves are opposite and mostly three-lobed.

ETYMOLOGY The species name *edule* lets you know the berries are edible. The Cree name for the plant is moosomin, which also forms the root of its other common English name, mooseberry.

HABITAT Open forests and forest edges at low to mid elevations.

FUNGI

RED-BANDED CONKS
Complex Fomitopsis pinicola

POLYPORE FAMILY Polyporaceae

ECOLOGICAL ROLE Red-banded conks are the fungal composters of Pacific Northwest forests. Appearing almost exclusively on conifers, they break down the trees' cellulose, creating a healthy soil additive and tree cavities for nesting birds and small mammals. The decayed soft pockets of wood allow easy access for woodpeckers in search of tasty insects. All wood rot fungi play important roles in the carbon cycle in the forest ecosystem.

DESCRIPTION The red-banded conk is known as brown crumbly rot to the BC Forest Service. Its perennial fruitbody is rounded, woody, and to over 60 cm (24 in.) across. The colours of this fungi can be variable; it is usually seen with a dark attachment to the tree and an orangey-red margin. The undersurface is white to off-white and extends to the outer edge. Red-banded conk is considered the most common conk in the Pacific Northwest.

ETYMOLOGY The species name *pinicola* means "pine dwelling." Long ago the word *pine* was synonymous with conifer.

The PNW is home to a dizzying array of shelf fungi, including the dyer's polypore (*P. schweinitzii*), sulphur shelf (*L. conifericola*), western varnish shelf (*G. oregonense*), and red-banded conks.

MARINE
PLANTS

BULL KELP
Nereocystis luetkeana

BROWN KELP FAMILY Laminariaceae

ECOLOGICAL ROLE Bull kelp forests supply a habitat and food source for more than a thousand species of marine life. Their long stipes and blades sequester carbon, which helps reduce acidification and ocean warming. In places where bull kelp is well established, the holdfasts, blades, and stipes mitigate the power of strong waves, reducing beach erosion. Healthy kelp forests are one of the most productive ecosystems in the world. Even when kelp is washed up along the beaches, it creates another ecosystem that feeds and protects crabs, molluscs, insects, and birds.

DESCRIPTION Bull kelp is one of the most recognized kelps in the Pacific Northwest and one of the largest, attaining lengths of over 30 m (100 ft.). The long brown stipe is kept afloat by a large pneumatocyst (float), which is decorated with over 20 blades, each to 3 m (10 ft.).

ETYMOLOGY The genus name *Nereocystis* is Greek for "mermaid's bladder."

HABITAT Grows on rocky areas in the lower intertidal zone, from Alaska to California.

MARINE EELGRASS
Zostera marina

EELGRASS FAMILY Zosteraceae

ECOLOGICAL ROLE Marine eelgrass forms one of the most diversified, important, and productive ecosystems in the PNW marine world. The grasses slow down the wave action hitting the beaches, reducing erosion. They act as filters trapping sediments, polluted runoffs, and organic matter and are carbon sinks. The long blades of grass are nurseries protecting small crabs, fish, invertebrates, and their eggs. Also, they are a very important food source for resident and migratory ducks, geese, swans, and herons.

DESCRIPTION Marine eelgrass has leaves to 1.2 m (4 ft.) long and 1 cm (0.5 in.) wide. A dwarf introduced eelgrass (*Z. japonica*) can often be seen growing with common eelgrass. The dwarf eelgrass has shorter, thinner leaves.

HABITAT Prefers protected bays and mud flats. Found from Alaska to Mexico.

LYNGBYE'S SEDGE
Carex lyngbyei

SEDGE FAMILY Cyperaceae

ECOLOGICAL ROLE Lyngbye's sedge is a pioneer species in that it is one of the first plants to colonize new or damaged silt tidal flats in the coastal PNW. Its powerful masses of rhizomes are invaluable for stabilizing silty soils in salt marshes and estuaries. The rhizomes are also an important food source for coastal grizzly bears, who will act as small excavators to access the roots. The smaller pieces of roots that the bears miss will float off at high tide and re-root elsewhere. The long leaves on Lyngbye's sedge act as water filters capturing all kinds of organic matter. They also play and important role in carbon sequestration. The sedges offer food, nesting, and protection to hundreds of species or marsh birds, shorebirds, raptors, ducks, and geese.

DESCRIPTION Lyngbye's sedge grows to 1 m (3.3 ft.). The leaves have reddish-brown sheaths; the inflorescence is stiff nodding spikes. It spreads by rhizome and is a favourite forage for grizzly bears, migratory geese, and trumpeter swans.

ETYMOLOGY The common name commemorates Hans Christian Lyngbye (1782–1837), a Danish priest and botanist who studied seaweeds.

HABITAT Found in mud flats, tidal flats, and salt marshes, from Alaska to California.

TREES

RED ALDER
Alnus rubra

BIRCH FAMILY Betulaceae

ECOLOGICAL ROLE Red alders are a pioneer species. They will quickly grow on avalanche paths, burnt-out areas, and freshly logged tracks of land. Their ability to convert atmospheric nitrogen into a form that is usable by other plants makes them one of the most important trees in the ecological circle. Under normal circumstances, conifers in the PNW will hold the land for 300–500 years. When they die from old age, fire, or insect attacks, the land is taken over by deciduous vegetation for 50–100 years. This change in vegetation puts much-needed compost and nitrogen from the alders back into the soil mix, letting the land recover and store organic matter, which will retain moisture. It also interrupts insects and soil-borne pathogens' life cycles.

DESCRIPTION The largest native alder in North America, the red alder grows quickly and can reach 25 m (81 ft.) in height. Its leaves are oval shaped, grass green, and 7–15 cm (3–6 in.) long with a coarsely serrated edge. Hanging male catkins, 7–15 cm (3–6 in.) long, decorate the bare trees in early spring. The fruit (cones) are 1.5–2.5 cm (0.75–1 in.) long; they start off green, then turn brown, and persist through winter. The bark is thin and grey on younger trees and scaly when older. Red alder leaves give a poor colour display in autumn, when they are mainly green or brown.

ETYMOLOGY The species name *rubra* refers to the bark, which shows red when it is scraped. The common name refers to the same.

HABITAT Moist wooded areas, disturbed sites, and stream banks at low to mid elevations.

CASCARA
Frangula purshiana

BUCKTHORN FAMILY Rhamnaceae

ECOLOGICAL ROLE When in flower, cascaras attract hummingbirds, moths, and most of the local bee species. The pea-like fruit feeds warblers, robins, band-tailed pigeons, jays, grossbeaks, tanagers, coyotes, and raccoons, while their leaves play host to the larvae of swallowtail butterflies and multiple moth species, which in turn are a food source for chickadees, bushtits, and kinglets.

DESCRIPTION Cascara can be a multi-trunked shrub to a small tree to 9 m (30 ft.) in height. Its leaves are oblong with prominent veins, glossy, grass green, and 7–13 cm (3–5 in.) long. The flowers are small, greenish yellow, and rather insignificant. The berries are 0.5 cm (0.25 in.) across and look like small cherries; they are red at first, turning bluish black in late summer. The smooth bark is silvery grey and resembles an elephant's hide on older trees. The bark was collected commercially for years and used as the key ingredient in laxatives.

ETYMOLOGY The species name *purshiana* commemorates Friedrich Traugott Pursh (1774–1820), a German-American botanist.

HABITAT Prefers moist, nutrient-rich sites in the shade of larger trees at low elevations.

SEASON The small flowers are produced in the spring, while the bluish-black berries are seen at the end of summer.

WESTERN RED CEDAR
Thuja plicata

CYPRESS FAMILY Cupressaceae

ECOLOGICAL ROLE Western red cedar plays an integral part in the ecosystem. The cedar's seeds are eaten by pine siskins and the foliage is browsed by deer and elk, while the trunks can be home to several species of birds and mammals. At the end of the tree's long life, the larger limbs and trunk can sit on the ground for hundreds of years without fully decomposing. In that time, they become nurse logs, supporting thousands of tree seedlings until they can grow on their own. The decomposing wood is extremely important to building up the litter and compost layers of the forest floor.

DESCRIPTION Western red cedar is a fast-growing large conifer with heights exceeding 60 m (200 ft.). Its bark sheds vertically and ranges from cinnamon red on young trees to grey on mature trees. The bases of older trees are usually heavily flared, with deep furrows. The egg-shaped cones are 1 cm (0.5 in.) long and green when young, turning brown and upright when mature (yellow cypress, in comparison, has round cones). The bright-green leaves are scale-like, with the appearance of overlapping shingles. Western red cedar is BC's provincial tree. On old stumps, springboard marks can be seen 2–3 m (6.6–10 ft.) above the ground. Early fallers used to stand on springboards when sawing or chopping the trees down; the springboards allowed them to get away from the tree's flared base. The shingle industry is now the biggest user of red cedar.

ETYMOLOGY The species name *plicata* refers to the new cedar shoots appearing to be plaited.

HABITAT Thrives on moist ground at low elevations. Will tolerate drier or higher sites but will not attain gigantic proportions.

DOUGLAS FIR
Pseudotsuga menziesii

PINE FAMILY Pinaceae

ECOLOGICAL ROLE Old growth or even second-growth Douglas fir forests in the PNW are like no other forests in the world. Their canopies support hundreds of species of animals, birds, plants, mosses, lichens, and epiphytes, while their annual shedding of needles and branches build a compost layer which supports berry bushes, fungi, ferns, and grasses. These in turn invite insects, birds, and mammals of all sizes, from mice and voles to cougars, deer, and bears. Douglas fir seeds are food to squirrels, chipmunks, mice, shrews, and many songbirds. Large plates of bark can sometimes be seen removed by bears accessing the sweet sap.

DESCRIPTION The Douglas fir is a fast-growing, tall conifer about 90 m (300 ft.) in height. Its bark is thick, corky, and deeply furrowed. The ovate cones are 7–10 cm (3–4 in.) long and have three forked bracts protruding from the scales; the cones hang down from the branches, unlike the cones of true firs, which stand up. The needles are 2–3 cm (1 in.) long and pointed at the apex, with a slight groove on the top and two white bands of stomata on the underside. It is the state conifer of Oregon.

ETYMOLOGY The common name commemorates the Scottish botanist and explorer David Douglas (1799–1834). The genus name *Pseudotsuga* translates from Latin to "false hemlock," an acknowledgement that this conifer doesn't quite fit in the neat box of nomenclature: it is not a true hemlock, fir, or pine, and stands as a unique entity of its own.

HABITAT Tolerates dry to moist conditions from low to high elevations. Reaches its tallest size near the coast.

BLACK HAWTHORN
Crataegus douglasii

ROSE FAMILY Rosaceae

ECOLOGICAL ROLE Black hawthorn berries, which ripen by mid-June, are a favourite for waxwings, blackbirds, redwings, finches, starlings, and black bears on their way to retire for the season. In areas where the hawthorns have been continually browsed by deer, elk, or in some cases, local sheep and goats, they form impenetrable thorned thickets that offer protection to small mammals and nesting sites for birds. Black hawthorns are larval hosts to pale swallowtail, western tiger swallowtail, and mourning cloak butterflies.

DESCRIPTION Black hawthorn is an armed, scraggly shrub or bushy tree that grows to 9 m (30 ft.) in height. The leaves are roughly oval, coarsely toothed above the middle, and to 6 cm (2 in.) long. The clusters of white flowers are showy but bland in smell. The edible fruit is purple-black, to 1 cm (0.5 in.) long, and hangs in bunches. Older bark is grey, patchy, and very rough.

ETYMOLOGY The species name *douglasii* commemorates David Douglas (1799–1834) a great plant collector and Scottish botanist.

HABITAT Prefers moist soil beside streams, in open forests, or near the ocean.

CALIFORNIA HAZELNUT
Beaked Hazelnut
Corylus cornuta ssp. *californica*

BIRCH FAMILY Betulaceae

ECOLOGICAL ROLE The nutritious hazelnuts, which ripen by August or September, have a community of followers, including deer, elk, woodpeckers, pheasants, squirrels, chipmunks, wild turkeys, quail, jays, ground squirrels, mice, and all other local rodents. The male catkins/flowers are a food source for ruffed grouse that depend on them at the end of winter.

DESCRIPTION California hazelnut is a broad spreading shrub 2–5 m (3.3–16 ft.) tall. The male flowers are formed in hanging catkins in early spring. Their pollen is mainly wind distributed to the small female flowers that have beautiful protruding red stigmas. A very close look is needed to see them. The toothed leaves are alternate, to 8 cm (3 in.) long, with a heart-shaped base. They give the forest a wonderful autumn-yellow colour.

ETYMOLOGY The genus name *Corylus* is from the Greek *korulus* [helmet], referring to the hard husk, while the species name *cornuta* means "horned."

HABITAT Open moist forests along the coast.

WESTERN HEMLOCK
Tsuga heterophylla

PINE FAMILY Pinaceae

ECOLOGICAL ROLE Western hemlock's ability to have its seeds germinate on dark forest floors make its seedlings important browse for snowshoe hares and rabbits, while the lower branches on mature trees are excellent browse for deer and elk. The dead trunks and branches from hemlocks decompose rapidly, making them key players in the forest soil ecology.

DESCRIPTION Western hemlock is a fast-growing pyramidal conifer to 60 m (200 ft.) in height. Its reddish-brown bark becomes thick and deeply furrowed on mature trees. The plentiful cones are small, only 2–2.5 cm (0.75–1 in.) long, conical, reddish when young, and brown when mature. The flat green leaves are 0.7–2 cm (0.25–0.75 in.) long. The ends of the branches (main leaders) and new shoots are nodding, giving the tree a soft, pendulous appearance that is good for identification. Western hemlock is the state tree of Washington.

ETYMOLOGY The species name *heterophylla* refers to the different lengths of needles on the same branch.

HABITAT Flourishes on the Pacific coast, from Alaska to Oregon, from low elevations to 1,000 m (3,300 ft.), where it is replaced by mountain hemlock (*T. mertensiana*).

BIGLEAF MAPLE
Acer macrophyllum

SOAPBERRY FAMILY Sapindaceae

ECOLOGICAL ROLE Bigleaf maples are food factories. Their millions of leaves nourish the forest floor with rich compost, feeding insects and microflora. The understory vegetation near or under bigleaf maples is very different in that it is more diversified than nearby conifer forests. The whirligig samaras seen in July are an important food source for squirrels, chipmunks, mice, and grosbeaks. The twigs are browse for deer and elk, while the entire canopy provides needed shade for salmon-producing creeks, streams, and rivers. The bark's moisture and calcium content supports epiphytes such as the licorice fern.

DESCRIPTION The bigleaf maple is the largest native maple on the west coast, often exceeding heights of 30 m (100 ft.). Its huge leaves, which are dark green, five lobed, and 20–30 cm (8–12 in.) across, are excellent identifiers. In early spring, it produces beautiful clusters of scented yellow-green flowers, 7–10 cm (3–4 in.) long. The mature winged seeds (samaras), 5 cm (2 in.) long, act as whirligigs when they fall; they are bountiful and an important food source for birds, squirrels, mice, and chipmunks. The fissured brown bark is host to an incredible number of epiphytes, most commonly mosses and licorice ferns.

ETYMOLOGY The species name *macrophyllum* means "big leaf." This species of maple has the largest leaves of any maple species in the world.

HABITAT Dominant in lower forested areas. Its shallow root system prefers moist soils, mild winters, and cool summers.

SITKA MOUNTAIN ASH
Sorbus sitchensis

ROSE FAMILY Rosaceae

ECOLOGICAL ROLE The late summer berries of Sitka mountain ash are a much needed mid-elevation food source for grouse, songbirds, small mammals, and if still available, for black bears. After consuming the berries, the songbirds will travel many kilometres dispersing the seeds. People should refrain from harvesting the berries and leave them for the wildlife that depend on them—the lower elevation European mountain ash seen all over cityscapes have excellent berries for picking.

DESCRIPTION Sitka mountain ash is a small multi-stemmed bush or thicket 1.5–4.5 m (5–15 ft.) in height. Its compound bluish-green leaves have 7 to 13 leaflets, 11 being the norm. The tiny white flowers are in terminal clusters, 5–10 cm (2–4 in.) across. From August to September, the bushes and trees display a wonderful show of bright red-orange berries. The bark is thin and shiny grey.

HABITAT Sitka mountain ash stays primarily where its name suggests: in the mountains. European ash can be found at lower elevations, especially near townships.

GARRY OAK
Quercus garryana

BEECH FAMILY Fagaceae

ECOLOGICAL ROLE Garry oak meadows support thousands of species of birds, mammals, insects, mosses, lichens, trees, plants, and grasses. The removal and fragmentation of them has meant the immediate endangerment of hundreds of plant and animal species. Already gone are acorn woodpeckers, western bluebirds, Lewis's woodpeckers, and streaked horned larks. Also, chocolate lilies, deltoid balsamroot, and Taylor's checkerspot are endangered as a result. In the autumn, ripe acorns are a favourite for black-tailed deer, bears, squirrels, woodpeckers, Steller's jays, and band-tailed pigeons.

DESCRIPTION Even when stunted or windblown, the Garry oak is the coast's stateliest deciduous tree. It ranges from 3 m (10 ft.) to 25 m (82 ft.) in height, and the male and female flowers are borne separately, but on the same tree. Like those of most white oaks, the leaves of the Garry oak are deeply round-lobed and to 12 cm (5 in.) long. (Red or black oaks have pointed lobes.) The acorns are 2 cm (1 in.) long, with a bumpy cap. The light-grey bark is tough, with thick edges.

ETYMOLOGY The plant explorer David Douglas, who was the first European to document the tree, dedicated it to his friend Nicholas Garry, deputy governor of the Hudson's Bay Company.

HABITAT Dry slopes and meadows on southeastern Vancouver Island, the Gulf Islands, and the San Juan Islands and elsewhere in Washington and Oregon.

SHORE PINE
Lodgepole Pine
Pinus contorta

PINE FAMILY Pinaceae

ECOLOGICAL ROLE Mainly seen along the coastal regions in the PNW, this is an important wildlife tree. Its oily seeds, when accessed, are a nutritional source to woodpeckers, chickadees, nutcrackers, crossbills, grossbeaks, jays, squirrels, and chipmunks. The foliage is browsed by grouse, elk, and deer, while the sap is enjoyed by porcupines and small forest rodents. Inspect empty bird nests where shore pines grow and you should find the outer structure made from pine needles.

DESCRIPTION Depending on where they are growing, shore pines vary dramatically in size and shape. By the shoreline, they are usually stunted and twisted from harsh winds and nutrient-deficient soil. A little farther inland, they can be straight-trunked and to 20 m (66 ft.) in height. The small cones, 3–5 cm (1–2 in.) long, are often slightly lopsided and remain on the tree for many years. The dark-green needles are 4–7 cm (2–3 in.) long and grow in bundles of two. The nuts are edible but small and hard to reach. Another variety, lodgepole pine (*P. contorta var. latifolia*), grows straighter and taller, to 40 m (132 ft.).

ETYMOLOGY The species name *contorta* refers to the tree's sometimes contorted shapes when growing by the ocean.

HABITAT The coastal variety grows in the driest and wettest sites, from low to high elevations.

WHITEBARK PINE
Pinus albicaulis

PINE FAMILY Pinaceae

ECOLOGICAL ROLE A high-elevation species, the whitebark pine has roots that help stabilize alpine soils. Their dense canopies retain snow-packs into summer, making water available to surrounding and lower-elevation vegetation. The canopies also shelter wildlife in winter's cold and summer's heat, while the seeds feed birds, squirrels, and grizzly and black bears.

CONSERVATION STATUS Endangered.

DESCRIPTION Whitebark pine can reach heights of 20 m (66 ft.), but it is often seen as a stunted bush under 3 m (10 ft.). Its needles are slightly curved, to 8 cm (3 in.) long, purplish when young, and green when mature.

ETYMOLOGY The species *albicaulis* means "white bark."

HABITAT Exposed dry sites at subalpine elevations. A related species, western white pine (*P. monticola*), can be seen at slightly lower elevations.

SITKA SPRUCE
Picea sitchensis

PINE FAMILY Pinaceae

ECOLOGICAL ROLE Sitka spruce are the guardians of the PNW's upper shorelines. In some cases, they are the front-line defence against fierce coastal storms, which is why they are often seen as gnarled short trees. Yet even 90 m (300 ft.) inland they grow to enormous heights. The tallest Sitka spruce are usually inland about 1.6 km (1 mi.), along salmon-bearing creeks. Their seeds, sap, and new shoots are an important food source for porcupines, Douglas squirrels, bears, rabbits, elk, and deer.

DESCRIPTION Sitka spruce is often seen on rocky outcrops as a twisted dwarf tree, though in favourable conditions it can exceed 90 m (300 ft.) in height. Its reddish-brown bark is thin and patchy, a good identifier when the branches are too high to observe. The cones are golden brown and to 8 cm (3 in.) long. The needles are dark green, to 3 cm (1 in.) long, and sharp to touch. Sitka spruce has the highest strength-to-weight ratio of any BC, Washington, or Oregon tree. It was used to build the frame of Howard Hughes's infamous plane, the Spruce Goose.

ETYMOLOGY The species name *sitchensis,* like the common name, refers to Sitka Island, Alaska (now known as Baranof Island).

HABITAT A temperate rainforest tree that does not grow farther than 200 km (125 mi.) from the ocean.

SCOULER'S WILLOW
Salix scouleriana

WILLOW FAMILY Salicaceae

ECOLOGICAL ROLE Willows are an integral strand in the web of life. They range from the boggy lowlands to the alpine tundra. Their male and female flowers are often the earliest to bloom, making their nectar a vital food source for moths, butterflies, mason bees, and honeybees. They are also larval hosts to eighteen different butterflies and moths. The branches and leaves are a browse for elk, deer, hares, and willow ptarmigan, and the bark is a favourite for beavers. Deep root systems and their love for water have made them invaluable for controlling soil erosion in riparian landscapes, such as creeksides, lakesides, and beaver ponds. Beavers will often build their lodges from willow branches, which root in the moisture and create green lodges.

DESCRIPTION Scouler's willow is a shrub or tree 5–12 m (16–40 ft.) in height. Its leaves are 5–8 cm (2–3 in.) long, felty, narrow at the base, and rounded at the tip. The flowers appear before the leaves; the males are to 4 cm (1.5 in.) long and the females are to 6 cm (2.5 in.) long. They can be found scattered in disturbed spots in young forests at low to mid elevations.

ETYMOLOGY The species name *scouleriana* commemorates Scottish naturalist John Scouler (1804–1871).

Native willows are easy to identify as a genus but hard to distinguish as a species. This is due to the variable leaf shapes within the same species, male and female flowers appearing on separate plants, flowering before leaves appear, and hybridization between species. The two most common willows are Pacific willow (*S. lasiandra*) and Scouler's willow.

ACKNOWLEDGEMENTS

This book could not be the quality it is without the help of many people, of whom I would like to acknowledge and thank the following: the University of British Columbia; Warren Layberry, who edited the manuscript; and the great staff at Heritage House Publishing, including editorial director Lara Kordic, editorial coordinator Nandini Thaker, and designer Rafael Chimicatti.

Having recently moved back to Vancouver Island, I wish to acknowledge that the land on which I now live and write is within the traditional territories of the Lkwungen (Esquimalt and Songhees), Malahat, Pacheedaht, Scia'new, T'Sou-ke, and W̱SÁNEĆ (Pauquachin, Tsartlip, Tsawout, Tseycum) Peoples.

BIBLIOGRAPHY

Clark, Lewis J. *Wild Flowers of British Columbia*. Sydney, BC: Gray's Publishing Ltd., 1973.

Harbo, Rick M. *Pacific Reef and Shore*. Madeira Park, BC: Harbour Publishing, 2006.

Haskin, Leslie L. *Wildflowers of the Pacific Coast*. New York: Dover Publications, 1977.

Hitchcock, C. Leo, Arthur Cronquist, Marion Ownbey, and J.W. Thompson. *Vascular Plants of the Pacific Northwest*. 5 vols. Seattle: University of Washington Press, 1955–69.

Lamb, Andy, and Bernard P. Hanby. *Marine Life of the Pacific Northwest*. Madeira Park, BC: Harbour Publishing, 2005.

Lyons, C.P. *Trees, Shrubs and Flowers to Know in British Columbia*. 1952. Reprint, Toronto: J.M. Dent and Sons, 1976.

Pojar, Jim, and Andy MacKinnon. *Plants of the Pacific Northwest Coast*. Vancouver, BC: Lone Pine Publishing, 1994.

Sept, J. Duane. *Common Mushrooms of the Northwest*. Sechelt, BC: Calypso Publishing, 2008.

Sheldon, Ian. *Seashore of British Columbia*. Edmonton, AB: Lone Pine Publishing, 1998.

Smith, Kathleen M., Nancy J. Anderson, and Katherine Beamish, eds. *Nature West Coast: A Study of Plants, Insects, Birds, Mammals and Marine Life as Seen in Lighthouse Park*. Victoria, BC: Sono Nis Press, 1988.

Stoltmann, Randy. *Hiking Guide to the Big Trees of Southwestern British Columbia*. Vancouver, BC: Western Canada Wildlife Committee, 1987.

Turner, Nancy J. *Plant Technology of First Peoples in British Columbia*. Vancouver, BC: UBC Press, 1998.

———. *Food Plants of Coastal First Peoples*. Vancouver, BC: UBC Press, 2000.

Varner, Collin. *Flora and Fauna of Coastal British Columbia and the Pacific Northwest* (Expanded Edition). Victoria, BC: Heritage, 2021.

INDEX

COLLIN VARNER began his career as a horticulturalist/arboriculturist at UBC in 1977, working at the Botanical Garden and, over the course of that career, assumed responsibility for conserving trees in all corners of campus, including those planted by graduating classes and ceremonial trees dating back to 1919. He retired in 2020. Varner is the author of *The Flora and Fauna of Coastal British Columbia and the Pacific Northwest* (Heritage House, 2018, 2021); *Edible and Medicinal Flora of the West Coast: British Columbia and the Pacific Northwest* (Heritage House, 2020, 2023); *Invasive Flora of the West Coast: British Columbia and the Pacific Northwest* (Heritage House, 2022); *The Flora and Fauna of Stanley Park* (Heritage House, 2022); *Gardens of Vancouver* (with Christine Allen); and a series of popular field guides, including *Plants of Vancouver and the Lower Mainland*, *Plants of the Whistler Region*, *Plants of the West Coast Trail*, and *Plants of the Gulf & San Juan Islands and Southern Vancouver Island*. He lives in Victoria, BC.